Chapter by Chapter Bible Study

James

All Books in the Series

Colossians

Ecclesiastes

Ephesians

Esther

Ezra

1-2 Peter

1-2 Thessalonians

1-2 Timothy

1-2-3 John / Jude

Galatians

Haggai / Zechariah

Hosea

James

Joel / Amos

Jonah

Lamentations

Malachi

Nahum / Habakkuk / Zephaniah

Nehemiah

Obadiah / Micah

Philippians

Ruth

Song of Songs

Titus / Philemon

CHAPTER BY CHAPTER BIBLE STUDY
James

An Easy-to-Use Study of
an Entire Book of the Bible

Troy Schmidt

Chapter by Chapter Bible Study: An Easy-to-Use Study of an Entire Book of the Bible—James
(VOLUME 16)

First edition
Printed June 2023

Printed in the United States of America

Cover design by David Hicks

For more information about the Author, go to www.troyeschmidt.com

ISBN: 9798399978376

Chapter by Chapter Bible Study

There are 66 books in the Bible. Some of them long, covering massive amounts of history. Some of them short and we wonder why they are there.

Christians believe every single word in the Bible is there for a reason, inspired by God. That means every book, every chapter, every word has a purpose.

Many studies are rich in details, drilling down deep into God's word. A small group can spend ten, twelve, fifteen weeks consuming thought-provoking wisdom every time they meet. That's a good thing, but these studies are different.

Inspired by CHAPTER BY CHAPTER: AN EASY-TO-USE SUMMARY OF THE ENTIRE BIBLE (Amazon), *Chapter By Chapter Bible Studies* tackle one book at a time, one chapter at a time, giving relevant attention to their history, meaning and application. It's everything you need to teach a thorough, complete and thought-provoking study, but at a slightly quicker pace.

Chapter By Chapter Bible Studies are formatted so easily they can be picked up at the last minute and taught comprehensively. Each study walks you through a chapter using a number of teaching tools:

- FACTS (context and background information)
- QUESTIONS (answers to difficult passages)
- DISCUSS (informative and fun interaction)
- FAITH (inspiring thoughts to motivate you)
- READ (a significant passage worth hearing)

But there's more to a bible study than just one meeting. Each *Chapter by Chapter Bible Study* provides a daily prayer guide for the teacher to use leading up to the study and for the student to use when the small group finishes, making sure the impact of the book continues for days to come. A Prayer Journal records prayer requests as a reference point to remember how God is working in lives of your people. There's even a fun quiz to test the class and see how well they paid attention.

Each *Chapter by Chapter Bible Study* inspires conversation, insight and application for the experienced and first time teacher to get the most out of each chapter of the greatest book ever written.

JAMES QUICK FACTS

Number of Chapters: 5
The Author: James the half-brother of Jesus
Approximately written: 46-49 AD (to Jewish Christians)

FACT: The name "James" referred to the half-brother of Jesus, born of Mary and Joseph, and once an unbeliever from Jesus' own family. He finally accepted Christ and became a leader in the church. (Not to be confused with James the brother of John and an apostle who was killed in Acts 12:2) James emerged in Acts 15 as a leader of the church in Jerusalem. This book was written to all Jewish believers (the twelve tribes).

FACT: James has been a controversial book because it emphasizes a faith that works. Many feel James was saying that someone must work to be saved, but that's not true. Martin Luther famously criticized James saying it was an "epistle of straw." He said Jesus was not mentioned in the book when, in fact, Jesus is mentioned twice (but not nearly as much as other epistles).

FACT: James could be the earliest book of the New Testament written between 45-50 AD, most likely before the Council of Jerusalem (Acts 15) which happened in 49 AD.

FACT: Some call James the "Proverbs" of the New Testament since it offers bite-sized, concise advice on how to live.

FACT: The book of James contains 15 indirect references to the Sermon on the Mount..

James 1

QUICK SUMMARY

James wrote to the twelve tribes (the Jews) among all the nations telling them to consider it joy when they face trials. These trials produce perseverance, leading to maturity of faith. Those who ask of God for wisdom should believe and not doubt. When tempted, don't blame God. The tempted allowed desire to give birth to sin, then sin leads to death. Be quick to listen, slow to speak and slow to be angry. Get rid of all moral filth. Don't just listen to the word, do what it says and don't forget it. Pure religion looks after orphans and widows.

FACT: James 1:1 – James wrote to the 12 tribes which means all Jewish believers in Jesus Christ. They were in many places, all around the world. The hope was that this letter would circulate.

READ: *Consider it pure joy, my brothers and sisters, whenever you face trials of many kinds, because you know that the testing of your faith produces perseverance. Let perseverance finish its work so that you may be mature and complete, not lacking anything. James 1:2-4*

DISCUSS: Is there a trial you faced that produced joy? (1:2)

FAITH: James 1:2 – We don't like trials. James said they're a good thing. Trials test our faith and make our faith stronger. Yeah, trials! Nobody prays for more trials but they can be a good thing.

QUESTION: **How can my trial produce joy? (1:2-12)**

Trials and joy don't seem to go together. We call something a trial because it doesn't bring joy, but heartache. But James says to look at it a different way. Look for the benefits that a trial produces. A trial forces us to look at ourselves and our circumstances differently. We have to rely on faith and put our trust, not in ourselves, but in God. James says that if we examine our trials carefully, they will produce:

1. Perseverance
2. Maturity
3. Wisdom
4. Dependence on God
5. Strengthened faith
6. Reduced doubt
7. Less expectation and more trust
8. Single mindedness
9. The crown of life

These are wonderful attributes causing us to almost want a trial in our lives so we can get more benefits. God can take any terrible situation and make it beneficial if we only trusted him. Jesus could not escape trials on this earth and he was God. We will face trials but it will all depend on how we view them: as annoyances or opportunities to grow.

DISCUSS: What's going on in your life that you need perseverance? (1:4)

FAITH: James 1:5 – Need wisdom? Just ask God. If you don't search for wisdom from God, you'll seek it from the world. That's a dumb decision.

DISCUSS: How is faithlessness like battling the ocean waves? (1:6)

FAITH: James 1:6 – Doubt is like sitting in a ship without an anchor. You'll drift wherever the wind and waves take you. Faith in God is in the anchor that keeps you securely in place despite the nasty weather.

FAITH: James 1:9 – The only "pride" a Christian should exhibit is in their humility. They are humbled that they have been deemed worthy of suffering for the cause of Christ. Oddly, pride and humility are completely opposite words.

DISCUSS: How can you have pride in your humble circumstances and it not be a sin? (1:9)

FAITH: James 1:12 – If you persevere and come out of a trial with your faith still intact (maybe even stronger than before), you will be blessed. The crown of life on the other side of your trial is the "carrot on the stick," the promise to keep you focused forward.

DISCUSS: How do you know if you're being tempted or tested? (1:13-14)

QUESTION: What's the difference between temptation and testing? (1:13-15)

A temptation is from the devil designed to make you do something against God's will. A testing is from God designed to make you mature and grow in your faith. God won't do anything to make you sin. That's the devil's work. God wants you to resist sin and grow stronger in your faith. His testing gives you an opportunity to choose sin or choose God. Satan only wants you to choose sin.

READ: *My dear brothers and sisters, take note of this: Everyone should be quick to listen, slow to speak and slow to become angry, because human anger does not produce the righteousness that God desires. James 1:19-20*

FAITH: James 1:19 – Best advice ever. Many of us don't listen, quickly saying something before we've thought about it and then getting angry before we know all the facts. James said mouth closed…ears opened.

DISCUSS: Are you a good listener? Why or why not? (1:19)

READ: *Do not merely listen to the word, and so deceive yourselves. Do what it says. James 1:22*

FAITH: James 1:22-25 – When you read the Bible, you are getting instructions from God. It's like looking in a mirror at yourself. God reveals your imperfections and your need for improvement. How is it that we walk away from the Bible and forget what the Bible says we look like? If you forget (or ignore) your sins you are saying God is not important, right or relevant.

QUESTION: Is there a problem if I listen to God and I don't do what he says? (1:22-25)

Many love to go to church and hear what the word of God says then exit the building and curse someone in the parking lot. Listening to God is the first step and very important, but our obedience is only complete when we put what we heard to use. James says a "listening-only" stance when it comes to God is not enough. In fact, he calls it deceptive because the person thinks he's doing something spiritual. A true follower of Christ listens, then "looks intently" at the word of God, then does it. That's where the blessing occurs.

DISCUSS: Why is looking after orphans and widows a sign of a healthy ministry? (1:27)

FAITH: James 1:27 – If you look after orphans and widows (or the homeless and abused), you are looking after people who can't do anything for you. Everything you do should be with that selfless mindset.

James 2

QUICK SUMMARY

Don't show favoritism to the rich. The poor are rich in faith while the rich exploit people and drag them to court. If you say you keep the whole law, yet stumble on one point, you break the whole law. Show mercy in your judgment. Your faith must be accompanied by deeds. You can't have one or the other. Even the demons believe and they shudder. Abraham had faith and offered his son as a sacrifice. Rahab had faith and hid the spies. Faith without deeds is dead.

DISCUSS: What would you do if a homeless man walked into church and sat next to you? What would you do if a celebrity walked into church and sat next to you? (2:1-4)

DISCUSS: How does someone show favoritism to rich people? (2:2)

DISCUSS: Can someone show favoritism to poor people? (2:3)

QUESTION: Is discrimination a sin? (2:1-4)

Discrimination, or favoritism as James calls it, is choosing one person over another based on their looks, income, status or what they can do for you. A homeless person can do nothing for you, so if you reject them on that reason, you are discriminating based on what's best for you and not what's best for that homeless person. Giving special attention to people based on your opinions is not right. We should judge people based on God's values—he created everyone and loves everyone. It's difficult sometimes when people act hateful and divisive, but we are commanded to love God and love others…no matter what they look like, believe or how they act. Racism falls under this category too.

FAITH: James 2:5 – While it's not always true, this principle is generally true. Poor people have more faith because they have less resources to trust in. Rich people have more resources so it's harder for them to trust what they don't see or what they can't buy.

QUESTION: Why am I guilty of breaking the whole law if I only stumble on one point? (2:8-10)

The goal of God's law is to show us that we are sinners. The law reveals that we are not perfect as God is perfect. How many laws has God broken? Not one. How many laws have we broken? Every one of them at least once, if not thousands of times. Adam and Eve committed one sin and became sinners, subject to death and cursed throughout their lives. The same applies to us. We want to grade on a scale, rating ourselves on how many sins we've committed compared to others. However, our model is not others, but Jesus, and with him as the model, we all fall short. Jesus committed zero sins. One sin and we're done.

FACT: James 2:10 – You don't *sort-of* break the law. It's pretty black or white. You either follow the law or not. 36 miles per hour in a 35 mile per hour zone is breaking the law. An officer in a speed trap may show you mercy if you go 36 but you're still breaking the law.

FAITH: James 2:12-13 – Don't judge. Show mercy. It's always better. Mercy is always better than judgment.

FACT: James 2:14 – This section in James caused some to believe this book should not be in the Bible (people like Martin Luther objected to it). Some believe James was saying that works save you. Not so. Our works are evidence of our salvation.

QUESTION: Why must my faith be accompanied by deeds? (2:14-18)

Imagine a person who says he is a sports fan but never goes to a game or watches a sport on TV or follows a specific team on Twitter. You would say that person is not really a fan. Why?

Because the person does nothing to support his words. The same is true for faith. If someone says they believe in God but they don't serve in a ministry, pay tithes, or go to church regularly, you would wonder if they truly believe. On the other hand, is it possible someone could go to church every week, serve in children's ministry and give when the plate is passed and yet not believe in God? Yes. Their faith is doing, not trusting. Good deeds can come before faith, but faith must accompany deeds because the word of God demands action.

DISCUSS: How can you really help a homeless person? (2:15-16)

READ: *In the same way, faith by itself, if it is not accompanied by action, is dead. But someone will say, "You have faith; I have deeds." Show me your faith without deeds, and I will show you my faith by my deeds. James 2:17-18*

FAITH: James 2:17 – James said that faith by itself, without any action, sounded like a dead faith. How can you say you're a Christian but never help anyone? Only a dead Christian does nothing for anyone else.

READ: *You believe that there is one God. Good! Even the demons believe that—and shudder. James 2:19*

DISCUSS: If demons believe, what does their belief lack? (2:19)

FAITH: James 2:19 – Demons believe in God. They see him! Yet they perform no actions to show they follow God. They have "faith" but no deeds. This verse challenges the idea of "belief."

QUESTION: Do the demons believe in God? (2:19)

Yes, but their "belief" is limited to what they see and know as fact. However, they do not put their trust in God and believe in God as the best for their lives. They don't surrender themselves to God and believe Jesus is their Lord. Believing starts with the truth of his existence, then motivates you to trust and surrender your life to him. Demons believe God exists but they don't surrender to him. Always make sure you define "belief" when talking to someone about God.

DISCUSS: What kind of deeds can one do believing their actions save them? (2:20)

FAITH: James 2:20-22 – Abraham was the best example of faith and deeds when he trusted God after God asked him to sacrifice his son. Abraham didn't just say "Yes Lord I'll do that one day." He showed his faith by going to the mountain and raising the knife over his son. God stopped him, satisfied Abraham had faith. His actions proved his faith.

FACT: James 2:25 – In the book of Joshua, chapter 2, a prostitute named Rahab hid two spies from the Israelites who were on a reconnaissance mission to plot the destruction of her city, Jericho. For Rahab, that took faith to trust the people who were there to destroy her city! Her faith was revealed by hiding and helping the spies get out of the city.

FAITH: James 2:26 – A heart monitor senses the pulse of a heart to determine if that body is alive or dead. A good deed monitor senses the pulse of a Christian's life to determine if they are saved or not.

James 3

QUICK SUMMARY

Not many should be teachers because teachers are held up to a higher standard. Everyone must watch what they say. A small bit can make a horse obey. A small rudder can steer a whole ship. A small spark can set a forest on fire. A small tongue can do a lot of damage. It's untamable. A poison. We can't curse and praise from the same mouth. A spring can't produce salt and fresh water. Likewise, you can't harbor bitter envy and selfish ambition. That's earthly and demonic. Sow in peace and produce a harvest of righteousness.

READ: *Not many of you should become teachers, my fellow believers, because you know that we who teach will be judged more strictly. James 3:1*

DISCUSS: If you were a teacher, what subject would you teach? (3:1)

FAITH: James 3:1 – Teachers have the power to sway their students towards God or away from him. If they teach anything contrary to the Bible, they will be judged for it by God. This should scare people away from the task for good reason.

FAITH: James 3:3-5 – Think of all the problems in the world that could have been solved if people kept their mouths closed. The tongue forms words sent from the brain either thoughtfully or emotionally. The mouth is the last defense against destruction.

DISCUSS: Are you good at controlling your tongue? (3:5)

READ: *All kinds of animals, birds, reptiles and sea creatures are being tamed and have been tamed by mankind, but no human* *being can tame the tongue. It is a restless evil, full of deadly poison. James 3:7-8*

QUESTION: **How do I watch what I say? (3:3-8)**

James said you had better watch what you say because the tongue is a terrible evil. "Taming" our mouths and what comes out of it is key to a peaceful life. James showed us how to do that:

- See the mouth as a bit or a rudder. Steer the tongue to say what's best to lead you in the right direction. Get control over it. Know that the tongue is a restless beast.
- Understand that the mouth can set terrible fires, with only a small spark. Douse the spark before it causes destruction.
- Do not inject poison into people's lives. That is done through opinion, gossip and lies.

Don't let your mouth destroy your life and the lives of others. Be slow to speak. Approve every word before it leaves your mouth. You do have the power to control your own tongue.

DISCUSS: **Have you been hurt by people's words? (3:7)**

FAITH: James 3:10-11 – Ask yourself, which does your tongue do more of...praising or cursing? It can't do both.

FAITH: James 3:13-14 – In the same way, a Christian can't do good deeds and selfish deeds at the same time.

FAITH: James 3:17-18 – Call this the fruits of wisdom—peace-loving, considerate, submissive, merciful, fruitful, impartial and sincere—similar to Paul's spiritual fruit list in Galatians 5, with some additions. A wise person should exhibit these qualities.

FAITH: James 3:17-18 – The first part of James 3 could be summarized as "talking the talk" while the second part could be summarized as "walking the walk."

James 4

QUICK SUMMARY

All the fights and quarrels occur in this world because of selfish desires and wrong motives. People want to be friends with the world and, in the process, they become enemies with God. So submit to God and resist the devil. Don't slander each other. There is only one judge who is able to save and destroy. Who are you to judge? Don't make your plans. Your life is but a mist. You should say, "If it's the Lord's will…"

DISCUSS: What was the last fight you had? (4:1)

FAITH: James 4:1-3 – All our fights and quarrels come from the same thing – we want something we can't have. Why don't we pray to God for it and let him decide what's best for us? Check your motive first.

FAITH: James 4:4 – You can't have two BFFs. To be the "best" means one is better than the other. We have to choose whether we want to be best friends with God or the world. One or the other. Who gets your priority?

QUESTION: What should my relationship with the world be? (4:4-5)

If you are in a relationship with God, then the world could be viewed as an adulteress. Why? Because the world demands that you love her exclusively while God demands the same thing. You can't truly be friends with two opposing sides. At some point, you have to reject one to show favor to the other. God wants you to love him and reach out to the world, pointing the world to God. The world wants you to love it and reject God, living as a worldly, sensual, pleasure-seeking person. God is jealous of your relationship with the world, because we wink and send flirty messages to the world all the time. God wants all your love because his love is best for you.

READ: *Submit yourselves, then, to God. Resist the devil, and he will flee from you. James 4:7*

DISCUSS: What does the devil think of you? What do you mean to him? (4:7)

FAITH: James 4:7 – Our resistance to the devil causes him to run away from us. He realizes it's futile to tempt you so he'll keep busy with someone else.

QUESTION: **How should I react to the devil? (4:7)**

Our response to the devil should be nothing. We should have no interaction with Satan. That's God's job. We should resist the temptations, then turn and walk away. No little conversations with his voice in our heads. No negotiations. Nothing. Many want to get up in his face and tell him off. You had better have the Holy Spirit inside you, totally submitted to God. There's really no need to engage with the devil. He's a dangerous tempter and has caused the greatest leaders to fall. You wouldn't go and pet a stray lion on the side of the road, would you? No, you would turn and walk the other way. Give all your focus to God and his powerful love for you.

READ: *Come near to God and he will come near to you. Wash your hands, you sinners, and purify your hearts, you double-minded. James 4:8*

FAITH: James 4:8-10 – James walks through a repentance process. We should grieve our sinfulness instead of shrugging and saying "oh well, I messed up again." Our sins should humble us before the Lord.

FAITH: James 4:10 – God desires to take your from your lowest moment to your highest. But we won't get there unless we are humble. God does not elevate arrogance.

READ: *Why, you do not even know what will happen tomorrow. What is your life? You are a mist that appears for a little while and then vanishes. Instead, you ought to say, "If it is the Lord's will, we will live and do this or that." James 4:14-15*

DISCUSS: If your life is a mist, what should you do today? (4:14)

QUESTION: How should I plan for tomorrow? (4:13-17)

We should be humble about tomorrow and flexible about God's plans. In the big picture we need to hold on to our lives loosely, ready for things to go any direction God determines. If our focus is on God's will then we can be more at peace. If not, our plans can turn into arrogant schemes—my way or the highway. The good we have to do is God's will. Then tomorrow becomes his day not ours. Our boasting then would only not be about how I used my time, but how God used my time on earth.

FAITH: James 4:15 – If life is short, then we should be in touch with the one who controls eternity. He knows how we can make the most lasting impact with what little time we have.

DISCUSS: What good have you done today? (4:17)

James 5

QUICK SUMMARY

James warned the rich. Their wealth had rotted and their corruption obvious. As for others, be patient until the Lord comes. Don't grumble. The judge is coming. Persevere like Job. Don't swear by heaven, just let your yes be yes and your no be no. If you're sick, let the elders anoint you with oil and make you well. Confess your sins and pray for each other. The prayer of a righteous person is powerful and effective. If anyone wanders from the truth, bring them back. You will save them from death and a multitude of sins.

DISCUSS: How rich do you wish you were? (5:1)

FACT: James 5:1-5 – James wasn't mad at all rich people, just concerned about those who put their faith in money and hurt anyone they can just to become richer.

FAITH: James 5:7-8 – We want Jesus to return NOW! But we must wait until the harvest is right or we'll ruin the crop. Our patience means more are hearing the Good News!

DISCUSS: Why do people grumble about you? (5:9)

FACT: James 5:11 – Job's perseverance while suffering brought about a double blessing in the end. Perseverance pays off.

QUESTION: How can I be a person of my word? (5:12)

"Swearing" in this sense means making an oath (not cursing at God). However, if we don't do what we say, then in God's eyes we are a curse (condemned). To be a person of our word we must do what we say we are going to do, plain and simple. If "yes" then do it. If "no" then don't do it. God keeps his word and follows through on every promise. We must do the same to be more like him.

DISCUSS: Have you ever had the elders of your church pray over you? What was that about and what happened? (5:14)

FACT: James 5:14 – The anointing of oil was symbolic of God's covering and blessing.

DISCUSS: Have you ever prayed for someone and they were healed? (5:15)

FAITH: James 5:15 – Will every person who is prayed for get healed? No. But the prayer is offered in faith meaning you're allowing God to do whatever he wants to do. Your faith is in him, not in the healing. You are trusting him to heal or not to heal.

READ*: Therefore confess your sins to each other and pray for each other so that you may be healed. The prayer of a righteous person is powerful and effective. James 5:16*

FAITH: James 5:16 – If you're a righteous person, that means you have the right relationship with God. Your prayers will be effective because you know the right way to pray, have the right faith and your relationship with God is very good.

QUESTION: Can we really pray for people to be healed? (5:14-16)

Jesus healed during his time of ministry on this earth. He came to show that God was all about wholeness. The deterioration of our bodies and mind begins with sin and selfish choices. "Wholeness" occurs when these bodies are free of sin. Is it possible to see healing as a result of prayer? Yes. It will always begin with prayer. Will everyone we pray for be healed? No. But it's possible they can be. We must always know that it's possible, if not, then why ask for healing? According to James, healing begins by asking for forgiveness and confessing our sins to one another. It's a spiritual healing from sin that is guaranteed. It's effective and what everyone needs.

DISCUSS: Why could confession lead to healing? (5:16)

FAITH: James 5:17-18 – It's difficult to think of a prophet like Elijah as a mere human being because of the extraordinary things he did. In 1 Kings 17 he prayed and all the rain stopped in Israel. In 1 Kings 18:44, Elijah said the word and rain started. James wants us to know that Elijah was flesh and blood just like us and if God could use him, he could use us.

DISCUSS: Have you ever led someone to Christ? (5:19)

FAITH: James 5:20 – We need to always challenge and encourage other believers making sure they don't stray from the faith. We must also go after those who have wandered from the flock of believers. Who knows, you could save them from death.

FINAL POINTS

1. Embrace trials.

Trials will come in your life. Don't be surprised. When they do come you have a choice—to fight, curse and grumble or to persevere, praise and learn. Trials are the best place to grow your faith and in your relationship with God.

2. Show your faith.

While our works do not save us, they are an indication that we have been saved. How do people know about Jesus in your life? Yes you can tell them but back that up by showing them too.

3. Watch your mouth.

The best advice in life is this: hold your tongue. You can avoid so many conflicts in this world by not saying, posting or tweeting on impulse and emotion.

QUICK QUIZ QUESTIONS

Q: James said we should consider it joy when we face what in our lives?
A: _____________ (James 1:2)

Q: James said we should be quick to listen but what two things should we be slow to do?
A: _____________ (James 1:19)

Q: Many who are poor in this world are actually rich in what way?
A: _____________ (James 2:5)

Q: A mouth shouldn't praise and curse just like a fountain can't produce what two kinds of water?
A: _____________ (James 3:10-11)

Q: We become an enemy to God when we become friends with what?
A: _____________ (James 4:4)

Q: What did James compare to a mist that appears for a little then vanishes?
A: _____________ (James 4:14)

Q: If someone is sick, who should be called to pray with them?
A: _____________ (James 5:14)

Time to Pray Through James

JAMES 1

READ: JAMES 1:1-11

Scripture focus:	*Consider it pure joy, my brothers and sisters, whenever you face trials of many kinds, because you know that the testing of your faith produces perseverance.* (1:2)
Time:	Around 46-49 AD
People:	God, James
Place:	To Jewish Christians
What's Happening:	James said to embrace trials because they make the believer stronger in faith. Ask for wisdom and don't doubt.

PRAYER

Dear God,
I will consider it joy when I face trials because I know that the testing of my faith only brings perseverance. Perseverance makes me spiritually mature and complete. I need to also receive more wisdom which only comes from You. You will generously give me the wisdom I need. But I can't doubt. I must believe so I can receive. I don't want to drift about in a storm of confusion. My faith is my anchor that holds true. I must be humble even if I find myself in a high position. Any high position can quickly dry up and fade away, humiliating me in the process.

KEEP PRAYING...
"Thank You for the trial of…"
"I need wisdom when it comes to…"
"I need to be more humble when I'm…"

I FEEL GOD IS SAYING TO ME...

JAMES 1

READ: JAMES 1:12-18

Scripture focus:	*When tempted, no one should say, "God is tempting me." For God cannot be tempted by evil, nor does he tempt anyone...* (1:13)
Time:	Around 46-49 AD
People:	God
Place:	To Jewish Christians
What's Happening:	God does not tempt. He tests. Temptation wants to drag the believer down. Christians can't be deceived.

PRAYER

Dear God,
Help me to persevere under trials. I want to pass the test so I can receive the reward, the crown of life You promise to all that love You. I need Your help to discern temptations from trials. You don't tempt. Temptation wants to drag me down and destroy me, giving birth to more and more sin and ultimately to death. I can't be deceived. This is too important. Every good thing comes from You. You don't change. You don't shift. Your truth is stable, reliable and fruitful in my life.

KEEP PRAYING...
"My biggest temptation is…"
"I'm getting stronger through the trial of…"
"You've given me the good and perfect gift of…"

I FEEL GOD IS SAYING TO ME...

JAMES 1

READ: JAMES 1:19-27

Scripture focus:	*Do not merely listen to the word, and so deceive yourselves. Do what it says.* (1:22)
Time:	Around 46-49 AD
People:	God
Place:	To Jewish Christians
What's Happening:	We must listen carefully especially to God's word. We must do what it says, never forgetting. By serving the least of these we are showing true faith.

PRAYER

Dear God,
I need to be a better listener. I need to say less. I need to stop getting so angry without all the facts. Anger doesn't make me righteous. I need to get rid of all the moral filth around me and all the evil that is so prevalent in my life. I must receive Your word, plant it in my heart and enjoy salvation. I can't hear Your word, then turn around and forget it. It's like forgetting who I am. Your word is the perfect law that gives freedom. If I do what the Bible tells me to do, I'll be blessed. I need to hold my tongue to hold on to my righteousness. If I don't, my religion is worthless. A pure faith is seen in my humble actions, serving others, especially the most needy. That keeps me from being polluted by this world.

KEEP PRAYING...
"When it comes to listening, I am…"
"When it comes to speaking, I am…"
"When it comes to serving, I am…"

I FEEL GOD IS SAYING TO ME...

____
____
____
____
____

JAMES 2

<u>READ: JAMES 2:1-13</u>

Scripture focus:	*My brothers and sisters, believers in our glorious Lord Jesus Christ must not show favoritism.* (2:1)
Time:	Around 46-49 AD
People:	God
Place:	To Jewish Christians
What's Happening:	Christians cannot show favoritism to the rich over the poor. James called it a sin.

PRAYER

Dear God,
Forgive me for showing favoritism. You don't show favoritism. You accept anyone who gives their life to You. I would have to ask myself how I would react if a big named celebrity entered a church service and a homeless person at the same time. Would I show preference and give my seat to the celebrity? It's the poor who are rich in faith. They have nothing else to trust and show incredible faith when they have nothing. The rich struggle with money, tempted by greed and lawsuits. Either way, favoritism is a sin. I am breaking the law by not loving my neighbor (both rich and poor) as yourself. I am going to be judged one day. I would want mercy shown to me. I need to start showing mercy to others. Mercy is always better than judging.

KEEP PRAYING...
"If a homeless person came into church, I would…"
"I show favoritism to the rich because…"
"To show mercy, I must…"

I FEEL GOD IS SAYING TO ME...

JAMES 2

<u>**READ: JAMES 2:14-26**</u>

Scripture focus:	*What good is it, my brothers and sisters, if someone claims to have faith but has no deeds? Can such faith save them?* (2:14)
Time:	Around 46-49 AD
People:	God
Place:	To Jewish Christians
What's Happening:	A Christians cannot say they are saved by faith and yet show no deeds. Even demons believe! James called that person's faith dead.

PRAYER

Dear God,
I must not only know my faith, but show my faith. A deedless faith is not a saving faith if I keep it inward and refuse to show it outward. A deedless faith is a dead faith. Faith must always be accompanied by deeds. Even the demons believe in You. They see You all the time! Yet, they don't have any good deeds to show by their belief. I must have the kind of faith like Abraham who took Isaac to the mountaintop willing to sacrifice him because You asked him too. He showed his faith by actions. Even Rahab showed her faith by righteous deeds, not just righteous thoughts. A body without the spirit is dead. So is my faith unless I do something.

KEEP PRAYING...
"The most recent deed I did was…"
"What keeps a demon from truly having faith is…"
"My faith is alive/dead…"

I FEEL GOD IS SAYING TO ME...

____

____

____

____

____

____

JAMES 3

<u>READ: JAMES 3:1-12</u>

Scripture focus:	*All kinds of animals, birds, reptiles and sea creatures are being tamed and have been tamed by mankind, but no human being can tame the tongue. It is a restless evil, full of deadly poison.* (3:7-8)
Time:	Around 46-49 AD
People:	God
Place:	To Jewish Christians
What's Happening:	James called the tongue fire and poison. A Christian cannot curse and praise with the same tongue.

PRAYER

Dear God,
I know that being a teacher is a powerful position that can lead many astray (and lead many to You). I must be careful with how I act, especially when it comes to my tongue. I want to be able to control what comes out of it. I want to steer my words towards blessing. It's such a small part of my body, but is it doing any good? With just the smallest wrong word I can set my world on fire. With just one sentence I can corrupt my whole body…the whole course of my life! Lions have been tamed, but can I tame my own tongue? I can't curse humans and praise You with this same mouth. It doesn't make sense.

KEEP PRAYING...
"Forgive me if I taught anyone wrongly…"
"Forgive me for what I've said to…"
"Forgive me for cursing with my tongue…"

I FEEL GOD IS SAYING TO ME...

____
____
____
____
____

JAMES 3

READ: JAMES 3:13-18

Scripture focus:	*Who is wise and understanding among you? Let them show it by their good life, by deeds done in the humility that comes from wisdom.* (3:13)
Time:	Around 46-49 AD
People:	God
Place:	To Jewish Christians
What's Happening:	True wisdom in a person's life would show itself through good deeds and the way one treats other people.

PRAYER

Dear God,
If I truly want to exhibit wisdom in my life, I would show it by my good deeds done in humility. Yes, wisdom and humility are the same thing. I cannot harbor envy and selfish ambition in my heart. I cannot boast about wisdom then turn around and deny it. That kind of wisdom is earthly and worldly, hellish and demonic. Envy leads to disorder and evil. I don't want to go there. Heavenly wisdom is pure, loves peace, is considerate to others, submissive to others, full of mercy, fruitful, impartial and from the heart. Wisdom finds peace to reap a harvest of righteousness. That's what I want.

KEEP PRAYING...
"Am I wise…"
"I find envy creeping in when it comes to…"
"My wisdom needs to be more…"

I FEEL GOD IS SAYING TO ME...

____
____
____
____
____
____
____

JAMES 4

<u>READ: JAMES 4:1-6</u>

Scripture focus:	*You desire but do not have, so you kill. You covet but you cannot get what you want, so you quarrel and fight. You do not have because you do not ask God.* (4:2)
Time:	Around 46-49 AD
People:	God
Place:	To Jewish Christians
What's Happening:	Our problems are rooted in our selfishness and friendship with the world. We should ask God what He wants for us.

PRAYER

Dear God,
All of the fights and quarrels that occur in my life come from my desires that rage inside me. I want something I can't have so I'll attack and hurt whoever stands in my way. I desire things that I can't have, so I pout and stomp my feet. I need to ask You if it's something I need or if it's something I should even pursue. I must check my motives for my desires. Is it for Your pleasure or my pleasure? I can't be friends with this world and stay friends with You. You are at war with this sinful world that pulls people's desires away from You. You put the Spirit in us to keep us focused on You. You oppose the proud and You love the humble. I must be more humble.

KEEP PRAYING...
"I find myself fighting with…"
"Forgive me for my desire to…"
"Forgive me for being a friend of this world…"

I FEEL GOD IS SAYING TO ME...

____
____
____
____
____

JAMES 4

<u>READ: JAMES 4:7-12</u>

Scripture focus:	*Submit yourselves, then, to God. Resist the devil, and he will flee from you.* (4:7)
Time:	Around 46-49 AD
People:	God, the devil
Place:	To Jewish Christians
What's Happening:	We have to resist the devil so he won't bother us. We are in control of our emotions. It starts with humility so we can remove our judgmental heart.

PRAYER

Dear God,
I submit myself to You. I vow to resist the devil and all his temptations to corrupt me and pull me away from You. If I make resistance to the devil a habit, he will run away, knowing that it's useless to try. But I must remain close to You and wash my hands of any wrongdoing. I need to kick out the evil thoughts in my heart.. I must be single-minded. I can control my emotions. They aren't in charge of me. I must turn that gloom into joy, my mourning to laughter. If I'm humble, You will lift me higher. And I can't go around saying bad things about my friends and family. Whatever I say is only judgment against them. You are the only judge so I don't have the right to judge anyone else.

KEEP PRAYING...
"I must resist the devil when it comes to…"
"I need to get in control of my emotions…"
"I have to stop judging __________…"

I FEEL GOD IS SAYING TO ME...

____

____

____

____

____

____

JAMES 4

<u>READ: JAMES 4:13-17</u>

Scripture focus:	*Why, you do not even know what will happen tomorrow. What is your life? You are a mist that appears for a little while and then vanishes.* (4:14)
Time:	Around 46-49 AD
People:	God
Place:	To Jewish Christians
What's Happening:	Life is so short. We should use this precious time to seek God's will and not our own.

PRAYER

Dear God,
Life is short. Yes I have plans and places I want to go, things I want to see. But what will that all matter? I want to find meaningful work and a nice living. But the truth is, I don't know what's going to happen tomorrow. I have no idea what direction my life will take. Life is but a mist that appears then dissipates before I know it. Gone. What difference does my will make when it comes up against someone else's will? Or Your will. I must seek Your will in all that I do. I don't want to boast about my selfish plans. That's evil. I should only boast about Your plans. I want to know Your good plan for my life. Once I know it, I must do it. If I don't, then that's a sin.

KEEP PRAYING...
"I have plans to…"
"But what are Your plans for my life…"
"I know what I need to do…"

I FEEL GOD IS SAYING TO ME...

____
____
____
____
____
____

JAMES 5

READ: JAMES 5:1-6

Scripture focus:	*Now listen, you rich people, weep and wail because of the misery that is coming on you. Your wealth has rotted, and moths have eaten your clothes.* (5:1-2)
Time:	Around 46-49 AD
People:	God
Place:	To Jewish Christians
What's Happening:	James condemned rich people who seek to hurt others in order to get richer.

PRAYER

Dear God,
Do I control my money or does my money control me? A rich person deals with many temptations, causing them misery. The love of money separates us from You. Everything on this earth will rot, corrode and get eaten by moths. Why put my faith in it? If I hoard money, wanting more and more, then I say it's more important than anything else on this earth. If I cheat people of their wages, then I don't consider their pain and my situation takes priority. The point of life is not to live in luxury and self-indulgence, but to serve others. I can't get fat on money. It'll just lead to my slaughter. I must love the innocent, not condemn them and murder them if they get in my way.

KEEP PRAYING...
"Forgive me for my greed…"
"If I were to get rich, I would…"
"I have hurt people to get rich…"

I FEEL GOD IS SAYING TO ME...

____
____
____
____
____
____

JAMES 5

READ: JAMES 5:7-12

Scripture focus:	*You too, be patient and stand firm, because the Lord's coming is near.* (5:8)
Time:	Around 46-49 AD
People:	God
Place:	To Jewish Christians
What's Happening:	James told the readers to be patient for the Lord's return. We can't grumble or swear falsely before His return.

PRAYER

Dear God,
I am impatient. I admit. I want things when I want things. I would be a terrible farmer, picking produce before it's ripe. I must stay calm through every season. One day You will return and nothing else will matter. So for now I must stand firm. I can't grumble about others, judging them because it'll only bring more judgement on me. I especially get impatient during times of suffering, but I should look at it as a time of blessing. Like Job, my suffering increases my perseverance, making me stronger in faith as I witness Your compassion and mercy. I leave it all in Your hands and swear by Your will, not mine. I must be a "yes" or "no" person – doing what I say I will do, no longer floundering in excuses.

KEEP PRAYING...
"I'm very impatient when it comes to…"
"Forgive me for grumbling against…"
"I need to do what I'd say I would do…"

I FEEL GOD IS SAYING TO ME...

____

____

____

____

____

____

JAMES 5

<u>READ: JAMES 5:13-20</u>

Scripture focus:	*Therefore confess your sins to each other and pray for each other so that you may be healed. The prayer of a righteous person is powerful and effective.* (5:16)
Time:	Around 46-49 AD
People:	God
Place:	To Jewish Christians
What's Happening:	James concluded the book by calling on the church to pray. Righteous people's prayers are very effective.

PRAYER

Dear God,
If I have a need, I must ask people to pray. If I have good news, I must tell it to others, especially in the family of God. If I'm sick, I must ask them to pray, even if it means the elders of the church must come and anoint them with oil. The prayers offered in faith, according to Your desire, will make the sick well and You will raise them up. I must confess my sins to one another so they can pray for me and I for them. That's where healing truly occurs – in a community of trust. I want to be a righteous person, like Elijah, whose prayers were powerful and effective. I need that community of believers to keep me in-bounds, not straying away and getting myself in trouble. I need others just like they need me.

KEEP PRAYING...
"I pray for the sick…"
"Am I a righteous person…"
"I pray for _________ who is straying…"

I FEEL GOD IS SAYING TO ME...

____

____

____

____

QUICK QUIZ ANSWERS

Q: James said we should consider it joy when we face what in our lives?
A: **Trials** (James 1:2)

Q: James said we should be quick to listen but what two things should we be slow to do?
A: **Slow to speak/slow to get angry** (James 1:19)

Q: Many who are poor in this world are actually rich in what way?
A: **Their faith** (James 2:5)

Q: A mouth shouldn't praise and curse just like a fountain can't produce what two kinds of water?
A: **Fresh and salt water** (James 3:10-11)

Q: We become an enemy to God when we become friends with what?
A: **The world** (James 4:4)

Q: What did James compare to a mist that appears for a little then vanishes?
A: **Our lives** (James 4:14)

Q: If someone is sick, who should be called to pray with them?
A: **The elders** (James 5:14)

WHAT I LEARNED FROM JAMES

PRAYER JOURNAL

GOD DESERVES ALL THE PRAISE FOR

____

____

____

____

____

FAMILY/FRIENDS/NEIGHBORS I AM PRAYING FOR

____

____

____

____

____

SALVATIONS I AM PRAYING FOR

____

____

____

____

____

MINISTRY OPPORTUNITIES I AM PRAYING FOR

HEALTH ISSUES I AM PRAYING FOR

NATIONS THAT NEED TO HEAR ABOUT JESUS

PRAYERS FOR MY COUNTRY

WHERE HEALING IS NEEDED

SACRIFICES I CAN MAKE

TROY SCHMIDT began writing animation in Los Angeles in 1985 (*Dennis the Menace, Heathcliff, Flintstone Kids*). In 1992, he moved to Orlando to write for *The Mickey Mouse Club* for three seasons. He adapted a Max Lucado children's book *Hermie* into a video, then created and wrote the future video installments and twenty Hermie books. Troy directed documentary footage in Israel for iLumina Gold, then returned in 2008 to host a documentary entitled "In His Shoes: The Life of Jesus" for GLO Bible software. Troy was also a producer for the GSN game show "The American Bible Challenge" starring Jeff Foxworthy and wrote the book and board game based on the show. He wrote two books for young men based on the Kendrick Brothers movies, "The War Room" and "Overcomer." Troy has served at Family Church in Central Florida since 1997 in a number of roles.

BOOKS

12 Truths & A Lie: Answers to Life's Biggest Questions (K-Love Books)
The Seven: Flood (Book 1) & Fire (Bood 2) (Brentwood)
How to Be a Superhero: Ten Superpowers God Gives You (Amazon)
The Whole Bible Story: Everything That Happens in the Bible (Bethany House)
Revealed (B&H Kids)
Fish Sandwiches: The Delight of Receiving God's Promises (NavPress)
The 100 Best Bible Verses for Mom (Amazon)
NIV Kid's Quiz Bible (Zondervan)
The 100 Best Bible Verses on Marriage, Family and Parenting (Amazon)
The 100 Best Bible Verses on Salvation (Amazon)
The 100 Most Confusing Verses in the Bible (Amazon)
Bible Trivia, Jokes & Fun Facts for Kids (Bethany House)
The Extreme Old/New Testament Bible Trivia Challenge (Broadstreet)
The Best 100 Bible Verses About Prayer (Bethany House)
The Best 100 Bible Verses About Heaven (Bethany House)
The 100 Most Encouraging Verses of the Bible (Bethany House)
This Means War: A Prayer Journal (B&H Kids)
The American Bible Challenge Daily Reader: Volume 1 (Thomas Nelson)
Chapter by Chapter: An Easy to Use Summary of the Entire Bible (Amazon)
Reason for Hope: Answers to Your Bible Questions (Amazon)
Reason for Hope: MORE Answers to Your Bible Questions (Amazon)
Reason for Hope: Answers to Your Questions about Heaven (Amazon)
40 Days: A Daily Devotion for Spiritual Renewal (Amazon)
Saved: Answers That Can Save Your Life (Amazon)
Release: Why God Wants You to Let Go (Amazon)
In His Shoes: The Life of Jesus (Amazon)
Laughing Matters (Lillenas Publishing)
Foundations: A Study of God (Amazon)
Living the Real Life: 12 Studies for Building Biblical Community (Amazon)

12 TRUTHS & A LIE: ANSWERS TO LIFE'S BIGGEST QUESTIONS

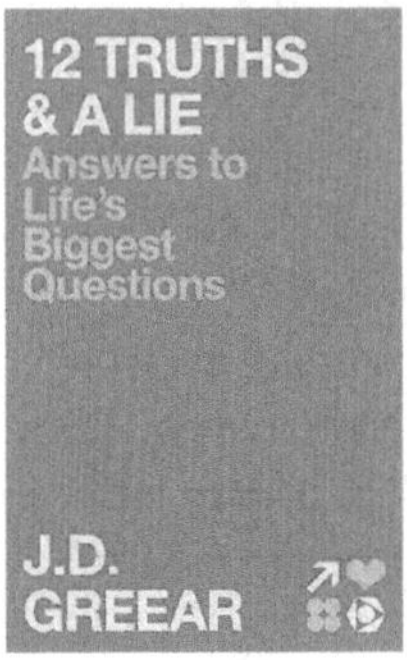

Life is full of difficult questions and many of them often seem impossible to answer. In *12 Truths and a Lie: Answers to Life's Biggest Questions* , author and pastor J.D. Greear confidently tackles some of the most perplexing questions that Christians face. A collaboration with author and pastor J.D. Greear

FISH SANDWICHES: THE DELIGHT OF RECEIVING GOD'S PROMISES

The Feeding of the 5,000 is the only miracle, besides the resurrection, mentioned in all four gospels. What was it about this miracle that every gospel writer felt they needed to mention? Fish Sandwiches (bread and fish) looks at 9 promises God communicated through that amazing miracle to apply to your life today and satisfy that hunger only Jesus can fulfill.

How to Be a Superhero: 10 Superpowers God Gives You to Make a Difference

God gives us the powers we need in the situations he determines. Walking through the Book of Judges, this book examines our God-given talents and personal uniqueness much like the superheroes of our day, both fictional and real. We can make a difference in a world desperately looking for heroes we can look up to. God can make you a superhero with the powers you already have!

THE 100 BEST BIBLE VERSES SERIES

The 100 verses that are highlighted include the well-known passages as well as hidden treasures. Each verse contains a brief devotional reading that will help you find comfort from the text, and in the process draw ever nearer to God. The book's length and focus make it perfect as a daily meditation or to read as a family. It also makes an ideal gift for those who love the Bible and seek the hope of God's promises.

REASON FOR HOPE:
ANSWERS TO YOUR BIBLE QUESTIONS

With over 50 answers to your Bible questions in every book, this book series answers some of the toughest questions people ask about God, their faith and the Bible.

IN HIS SHOES: THE LIFE OF JESUS

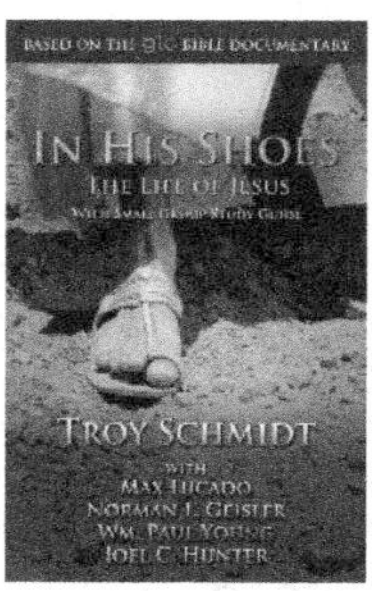

IN HIS SHOES: THE LIFE OF JESUS journeys to the all the places Jesus visited, from birth to death to resurrection and ascension. To help him along in his journey, Troy met up some of the greatest thinkers and writers from diverse perspectives to help him understand the experience (Max Lucado, Norman Geisler, William Paul Young, Joel Hunter and Avner Goren). The book includes a chapter-by-chapter Study Guide for Small Groups to use with the documentary which is available on the Glo Bible.

100 BEST BIBLE VERSES ON SALVATION

This book examines the 100 best Bible verses from the New Testament that explain clearly what salvation through Jesus Christ is all about. Includes additional chapters from Troy's book "Saved" to help the reader understand even more clearly what it means to accept Christ. Perfect for new believers and seekers.

100 BEST BIBLE VERSES ON MARRIAGE, FAMILY & PARENTING

A complete summary of all the best verses on the family, perfect for newlyweds, new parents or people who just want to strengthen their marriage. No other institution is under greater attack these days than the family. Discover God's best for all your relationships.

100 BEST BIBLE VERSES FOR MOM

A book of biblical encouragement including verses to help every mom get through her day and show her that God appreciates her role in giving life to her family. The ideal gift to your love to your mom.

100 MOST CONFUSING VERSES IN THE BIBLE

Easy to understand answers of the 100 most confusing, sometimes bizarre, passages we read in the Bible, explained with easy to understand answers.

CHAPTER BY CHAPTER: AN EASY-TO-USE SUMMARY OF THE ENTIRE BIBLE

The Bible is an intimidating book. It's easy to get lost in its pages. We all, sometimes, just need a little help to navigate through its pages. CHAPTER BY CHAPTER walks you through the Bible so that you understand all 929 chapters of the Old Testament and all 260 chapters of the New Testament. This book is not meant to replace your reading of God's word but it is useful as a reference guide to understand what you are reading or where to find passages and stories you know are in the Bible. It's time to begin your study of the entire Bible...chapter by chapter.

My number ONE seller on Amazon! Available on Kindle too.

The Whole Bible Story: Everything that Happens in the Bible

This young reader's edition of *The Whole Bible Story* will help you understand what the stories in the Bible are actually all about and how every single one of them fits together to tell one big story about God and his love for people--even you!

Along with the story of the Bible in words you can easily understand, in every chapter you will find great bonus material like exciting illustrations, fun facts and trivia about the Bible stories, simple lists of important characters and places, and easy-to-follow ways to apply the themes to your own life.

SAVED: ANSWERS THAT CAN SAVE YOUR LIFE

SAVED answers 25 questions that many ask before they find God—good questions, tough questions—that drown many in doubt and confusion before they find the answers. Questions such as: Do you have to know the Bible to be saved? Why was Jesus crucified? Is Christianity the only true faith? Don't we have to believe and do good works? Is the Trinity one God or three? How are those who never hear the Gospel saved? How am I saved?

RELEASE: WHY GOD WANTS YOU TO LET GO

Jesus focused on the concept of releasing. He told people to let go of things all the time. Why do we need to know that today? Our hands are so full that we can't receive God's blessing. Our grip is so tight that we can't grab on to what really matters. RELEASE explores this concept found throughout the Gospels – what was released and what the person received in return. From the characters in the parables to the real people in Jesus' life, we'll see that releasing our lives actually fills our lives.

40 DAYS: A DAILY DEVOTION FOR SPIRITUAL RENEWAL

40 is a very significant number in the Bible, especially when it comes to 40 days. Some of most significant characters of the Old and New Testament had experiences that lasted 40 days—Noah, Moses, Joshua, David, Elijah, Ezekiel, Jonah, Jesus. What happened during that time and what did it take 40 days for them to experience? Renewal.
40 DAYS examines their life-changing encounters and draws from their lessons of transformation using 40 daily devotions you can use for your own renewal experience. It worked for them...why not you. After 40 days, you'll come back as good as new.

KID'S QUIZ BIBLE

This full-feature Bible for ages 8-12 offers children a challenging experience as they delve into the Bible. Highlighting important facts and verses, the *NIV Kids' Quiz Bible* helps children engage with the text, while making it fun to learn all about God's Word! With answers to find in every book of the Bible, they won't want to stop reading. (Zondervan)

THIS MEANS WAR: A STRATEGIC PRAYER JOURNAL

The teen years can be tough; don't try to make it through without one of your most powerful weapons—prayer. A companion book to the movie *War Room,* this new kind of journal will get you ready for a new kind of prayer life, one that's strong, growing, and reflects just how powerful prayer is. Each short chapter tackles one of the biggest questions teens have about prayer. Just-right journaling prompts will then get you thinking—and praying—and reinforce the real power of fighting battles on your knees.

THE AMERICAN BIBLE CHALLENGE DAILY READER

In fall 2012, a new show premiered on the Game Show Network that quickly surprised Hollywood. Hosted by Jeff Foxworthy, *The American Bible Challenge* built up an audience of 2.3 million viewers in just nine weeks, making it the highest-rated show ever in GSN history. Now, the producer for the show, Troy Schmidt, with a foreword written by host Jeff Foxworthy, has released a daily reader based on *The American Bible Challenge* designed to take us deeper into the questions from the show and the life applications that they inspire.

PRAYING THROUGH THE BIBLE SERIES

PRAYING THROUGH THE BIBLE SERIES takes the reader through written prayers, with additional prompts to help you continue a focused time for prayer based on the passages. There is also space to record what God is saying to you during your time with Him. By the end, you will have prayed through God's word and gained a deeper appreciation for the Bible.

THE EXTREME OLD TESTAMENT / NEW TESTAMENT BIBLE TRIVIA CHALLENGE

Over 6,000 questions, written in the order as they appear in the Bible – from Genesis to Revelation. One question appears from EVERY chapter in the Bible. Great to use for a personal or group fun, for long car trips or morning devotions. Get to know the Bible in a fun and challenging way.

REVEALED

A young man's devotional based on the Kendrick Brother's movie "Overcomer." Written to help a young man discover God's intention and design in making each every one of us, "Revealed" dives deep into the best scriptures to allow the reader to his uniqueness and perfection in God's eyes. Written with Stephen and Alex Kendrick.

THE SEVEN:
FLOOD (Book 1) / FIRE (Book 2) / DARKNESS (Book 3)

A biblical fiction series following 7 young adults endowed with certain spiritual abilities as they travel through time to stop an enemy from disrupting biblical history. Their encounters put them right in the middle of the Bible's most incredible miracles.

THE GREATEST QUOTES JESUS EVER SAID
THE GREATEST QUESTIONS JESUS EVER ASKED
A 100 Day Devotional

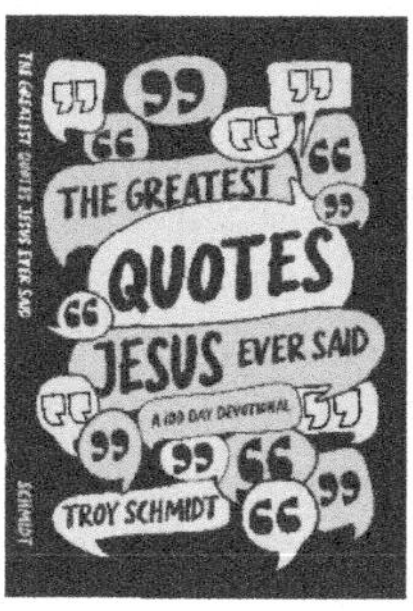

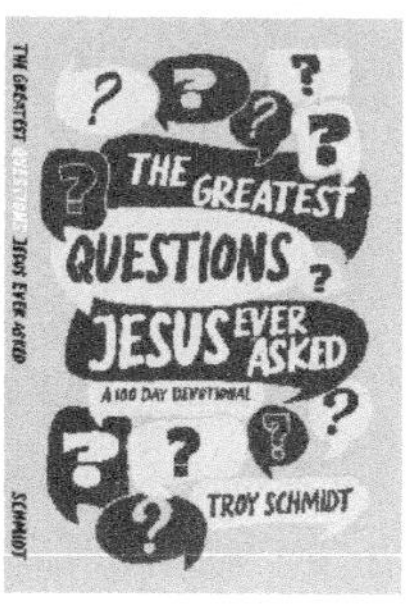

Begin every day with an inspirational thought and a life-changing challenge in these two daily devotionals that examine the best quotes and questions spoken by Jesus himself. (Amazon)

Made in the USA
Columbia, SC
02 June 2025

58841597R00030